Twenty to Knit

Knitted Baby Mittens

Sian Brown

Search Press

Dedication

For my daughters Hannah and Rhiannon; with happy memories of them being small enough to wear these, and for their ongoing interest and support.

First published in Great Britain 2017

Search Press Limited
Wellwood, North Farm Road,
Tunbridge Wells, Kent TN2 3DR

Text copyright © Sian Brown 2017

Photographs by Fiona Murray

Photographs and design copyright
© Search Press Ltd. 2017

ISBN: 978-1-78221-239-3

Publisher's Note

The Publishers and author can accept no responsibility for any consequences arising from the information, advice or instructions given in this publication.

Readers are permitted to reproduce any of the items in this book for their personal use, or for the purposes of selling for charity, free of charge and without the prior permission of the Publishers. Any use of the items for commercial purposes is not permitted without the prior permission of the Publishers.

Suppliers

If you have difficulty in obtaining any of the materials and equipment mentioned in this book, then please visit the Search Press website for details of suppliers:
www.searchpress.com

Printed in China

Contents

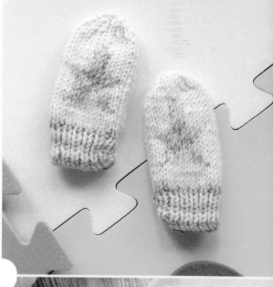

Introduction

Hand-knitted mittens have long been popular accessories to make for babies and small children. Whether they are a gift for a newborn, or a fun present for an older toddler, they make great projects to knit and give to friends and family.

The mittens are easy to make, use very little yarn, and are a good way to use up oddments or leftover yarn in your stash. They are quick enough to knit as the little one gets bigger, or if you would like to replace lost ones.

I have designed 20 pairs of mittens in three different sizes: 0–3 months, 3–6 months and 6–12 months old, all of which are suitable for both boys and girls, and cover a wide variety of techniques and styles. These include texture, cable, lace, Fair Isle, intarsia and embroidery – so there's something for everyone.

The smaller pairs of mitts without thumbs need only simple decreasing, so can be made easily by beginners looking for a light and uncomplicated project. The largest mitten size has incorporated thumbs, and instructions for these are included separately in the patterns.

Happy knitting!

Knitting know-how

Multicoloured techniques

Fair Isle Make sure the strands at the back of the work are pulled tightly enough to stop little fingers getting caught, but not too tight to pull in the work.

Intarsia Before starting, wind off small amounts of yarn for each area of colour in the motif. Twist the yarn at the back of the work when changing colour.

Magic loop method

The magic loop is a good technique to use when you have a small number of stitches and a small circumference to knit on circular needles. Take care to not get the stitches twisted around the needles at any point.

1 Cast on the required number of stitches onto your circular needle.

2 Move all the stitches to the centre of the flexible part of the needle (the cable), then find the approximate centre point for the stitches.

3 Divide the work into two, then gently push the two sets of stitches apart and back onto the needles, creating a loop shape on the cable. This should be on your left. Make sure that the stitches do not twist – this is very important, as if they do you will need to begin again.

4 Hold the needles parallel to your body, with one in front of the other, so that the needle with the stitches first cast on is closest to you. Put the working yarn over the back needle if the first stitch is a k stitch, or between the needles nearest to you if it is a p stitch.

5 Push the stitches on the back needle back onto the cable. Do this by gripping the point of the needle, and gently pulling it to the right then forward. Position your needle in the first stitch ready to knit. You should now have a loop of cable also on your right.

6 Begin to knit the stitches, knitting across the first needle.

7 To turn the work, turn the needles so that the unworked stitches are now nearest to you. Pull the stitches at the back onto the cable needle in the same way as before (**5**). These are the ones just worked. Keeping the working yarn towards the back, bring the back needle around and prepare to k the first stitch.

8 Once this second set of stitches have been worked, one round has been completed. It is useful to place a marker here, so that are easily able to recognise he beginning of a new round. Continue until the number of rounds have been worked according to the pattern.

Size

The three sizes have been laid out in the patterns with the smallest first and the larger two following in brackets: 0–3(3–6:6–12) months.

Tension

As the mittens need to be a good fit, the finished measurements are important. If you can't get the correct tension, change the needle size until you do.

Sewing up

Break yarn, leaving long tails to thread through remaining stitches with a tapestry (blunt-end) needle. Pull top of mittens tight and weave in the ends.

Making a plaited tie

Cut the lengths of yarn as the pattern suggests. Tie a knot in one end and plait to form a tie. Secure at the end with a second knot and trim the ends of the strands of yarn.

Embroidery stitches

Some designs in this book feature embroidery, including a back stitch and the three stitches below.

French knot

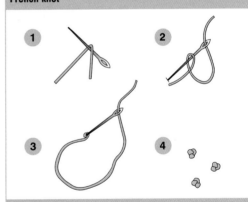

Chain stitch

Lazy daisy

Abbreviations

The abbreviations listed below are the most frequently used terms in the book.
Any special abbreviations in a pattern are explained on the relevant page.

DPN	double-pointed needles	**p2tog**	purl 2 stitches together
k	knit	**psso**	pass slip stitch over
k2tog	knit 2 stitches together	**rep**	repeat
k2togtbl	knit 2 stitches together through back loop	**ssk**	slip 2 stitches knitwise one at a time
m1	make 1 stitch by lifting bar of yarn before next stitch with the left needle, and then knitting into the back of loop	**sl**	slip stitch
		sm	slip marker
		st	stitch
p	purl	**st st**	stocking/stockinette stitch
patt	pattern	**tbl**	through back of loop
		yo	yarn over

Materials:

4-ply (fingering) weight yarn
  Yarn A: 1 x 50g (1.75oz) ball, cream
  Yarn B: small amount, turquoise
  Yarn C: small amount, violet
  Yarn D: small amount, grey

2 stitch markers

Stitch holder

Needles:

Set of 3mm (UK 11/US 2) DPN, or a 3mm (UK 11/US 2)
  circular needle

Tapestry (blunt-end) needle for sewing up

Tension:

32 sts x 36 rounds = 10cm/4in over Fair Isle pattern
  using 3mm (UK 11/US 2) needles

Chart:

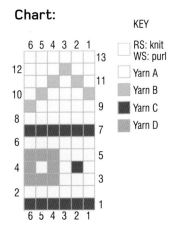

KEY

☐ RS: knit
   WS: purl
☐ Yarn A
▨ Yarn B
■ Yarn C
▨ Yarn D

Sizes 0–3 months and 3–6 months only

Continue to work as set until 2 reps of the 13th round on chart are complete, and then work round 1 once more.

Work 0(3) rounds in yarn A only.

Size 6–12 months only

Starting with round 2 of the Fair Isle chart, work 4 rounds of chart as set.

Next round: patt 21, place marker, m1 in yarn A, place marker, patt to end. (43 sts)

Next round: patt to end, slipping markers and working sts between markers in yarn C.

Next round: patt to marker, sm, m1, k to marker in yarn A, m1, sm, patt to end. (45 sts)

Next round: patt to end, slipping markers and working sts between markers in yarn A.

Repeat last 2 rounds until there are 13 sts between markers, working sts between markers in yarn A, except for chart rounds 1 and 7; these should be worked in yarn C to continue stripe. (55 sts)

Next round: k to marker, remove marker, place 13 sts from between markers on holder, k to end. (42 sts)

Continue to work as set until 2 reps of the 13th round chart are complete, and then work rounds 1–7 once more.

Work 1 round in yarn A only.

All sizes

Continue in yarn A only.

Next round: (k2tog, k2) to last 2(0:2) sts, k2tog(0:k2tog). (22(27:31) sts)

Next round: k.

Next round: (k1, k2tog) to last 1(0:1), k1(0:1). (15(18:21) sts)

Next round: (k2tog) to last 1(0:1), k1(0:1). (8(9:11) sts)

Next round: (k2tog) to last 0(1:1), k0(1:1).

Break yarn and follow *Sewing up* instructions on page 6.

Instructions:

These mittens are worked in the round using either double-pointed needles, or a circular needle and the magic loop method.

Make two.

Cast on 28(36:40) sts using yarn B and 3mm (UK 11/US 2) DPN or a 3mm (UK 11/US 2) circular needle, then join in the round, taking care not to twist stitches.

Change to yarn A.

Round 1: (k2, p2) to end.

Repeat round 1 six(six:seven) more times.

Next round: rib 9(36:13), m1(0:1), rib 10(0:14), m1(0:1), rib to end. (30(36:42) sts)

Continue in st st (k all sts) for rest of pattern.

Next round: work Fair Isle chart five(six:seven) times.

Thumb, size 6–12 months only

Place 13 sts from holder onto a 3mm (UK 11/US 2) needle.

With RS facing, using yarn A, pick up and knit 1 st from thumb gap before sts on needle/s; knit 13 sts from needle and arrange in the round. (14 sts)

Work 5 rounds in st st.

Next row: (ssk) three times, (k2tog) four times. (7 sts)

Break yarn and thread through remaining sts, pull tight and secure. Weave in ends.

Lace Border

Materials:

Baby – between 4-ply (fingering) and DK (US sport)
   weight yarn
   1 x 50g (1.75oz) ball, pink

2 stitch markers

Stitch holder

Needles:

Set of 3mm (UK 11/US 2) DPN, or a 3mm (UK 11/US 2)
   circular needle

Tapestry (blunt-end) needle for sewing up

Tension:

25 sts x 34 rounds to 10cm/4in over st st using 3mm
   (UK 11/US 2) needles

Instructions:

These mittens are worked in the round using either
double-pointed needles, or a circular needle and the
magic loop method

Make two.

Cast on 24(28:32) sts using pink yarn and 3mm (UK 11/
US 2) DPN or a 3mm (UK 11/US 2) circular needle, then
join in the round, taking care not to twist stitches.

Round 1 (RS): (k1, p1) repeat to end.

Round 2: (k1, p2tog, yo, p1) repeat to end.

Repeat rounds 1 and 2 twice(twice:three times) more and
then round 1 once more.

Next round: k.

Next round: (k1, k2tog, yo, k1) repeat to end.

Sizes 0–3 months and 3–6 months only

Continue in st st until mitten measures 9(10)cm/3½(4)in
from cast-on edge.

Size 6–12 months only

Work 1 round in st st.

Continue in st st (k all rounds) for rest of mitten.

Next round: k16, place marker, m1, place marker, k to end.
(33 sts)

Next round: k to end, slipping markers.

Next round: k to marker, sm, m1, k to marker, m1, sm, k to
end. (35 sts)

Repeat last 2 rounds four more times, until there are 11 sts.
(43 sts)

Next row: k to marker, remove marker, place 11 sts from
between markers on holder, remove marker, k to end.
(32 sts)

Continue in st st until mitten measures 11cm/4¼in from
cast-on edge.

All sizes

Next round: (k2, k2tog) to end. (18(21:24) sts)

Next round: k.

Next round: (k1, k2tog) to end. (12(14:16) sts)

Next round: k2tog to end. (6(7:8) sts)

Break yarn and follow *Sewing up* instructions on page 6.

Thumb, size 6–12 months only

Place 11 sts from holder onto a 3mm (UK 11/US 2) DPN or
circular needle.

With RS facing, using pink yarn, pick up and knit 1 st from
thumb gap before sts on needle/s; knit 11 sts from needle
and arrange in the round. (12 sts)

Work 3 rounds in st st.

Next row: (ssk) three times, (k2tog) three times.

Break yarn, thread through remaining stitches, pull tight and
secure. Weave in ends.

Tie
Make two.

Cut six strands of yarn 50cm/20in long. Plait to form a tie,
and thread through the top of the lace border.

Anchor

Materials:

4-ply (fingering) weight yarn
    Yarn A: 1 x 50g (1.75oz) ball, cream
    Yarn B: small amount, denim
    Yarn C: small amount, red

2 stitch markers

Stitch holder

Chart:

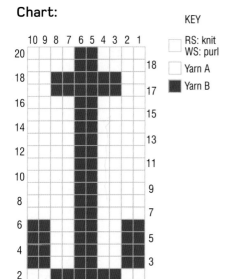

KEY

☐	RS: knit WS: purl
☐	Yarn A
■	Yarn B

Instructions:

Knitted flat.

Make two.

Cast on 26(32:36) sts using yarn B and 3mm (UK 11/US 2) needles.

Row 1: k2(0:0), (p2, k2) to end.

Row 2: (p2, k2) to last 2(0:0) sts, p2(0:0).

Repeat rows 1 and 2 four more times, working stripes as follows: 2 rows in yarn A, 2 rows in yarn C, 2 rows in yarn A, 2 rows in yarn B.

Change to 3.25mm (UK 10/US 3) needles and yarn A.

Row 11 (RS): k6(8:9), m1, k7(8:9), m1, k6(8:9), m1, k7(8:9). (29(35:39) sts)

Row 12: p.

Continue in st st for rest of pattern.

Needles:

2 pairs – 3mm (UK 11/US 2) and 3.25mm (UK 10/US 3) needles

Tapestry (blunt-end) needle for sewing up

Tension:

28 sts x 36 rows = 10cm/4in, over st st using 3.25mm (UK 10/US 3) needles

Sizes 0–3 months and 3–6 months only

Starting with row 1 of the Anchor chart, work as follows:

Row 13: k2(4), work chart, k to end in yarn A.

Row 14: p17(21), work chart, p to end.

Continue as set until chart is complete, ending with a purl row.

Continue in yarn A and st st for 0(2) rows.

Size 6–12 months only

Continue in yarn A.

Work 2 more rows in st st.

Starting with row 1 of the Anchor chart, work as follows:

Row 15: k5, work chart, k4, place marker, m1, k1, m1, place marker, k to end in yarn A. (41 sts)

Row 16: p to marker, sm, p to marker, sm, p4, work chart, p to end.

Row 17: k5, work chart, k4, sm, m1, k to marker in yarn A, m1, sm, k to end. (43 sts)

Row 18: p to marker, sm, p to marker, sm, p4, work chart, p to end.

Repeat last 2 rows four more times, until there are 13 sts between markers. (51 sts)

Row 27: k5, work chart, k4, remove marker, place 13 sts from between markers on holder, cast on 1 st, remove marker, k to end. (39 sts)

Continue in st st until chart is complete, ending with a purl row.

Work 2 rows in yarn A only.

All sizes

Continue in yarn A.

Next row: k2(3:4), (ssk) twice, k2(4:6), (k2tog) twice, k1(3:5) twice, k1. (19(27:31) sts)

Next row: p.

Next row: k2(1:1), ssk(ssk twice:ssk twice), k2(2:4), k2tog (k2tog twice:k2tog twice), k3(5:5), ssk(ssk twice:ssk

twice), k2(2:4), k2tog(k2tog twice:k2tog twice), k2(1:1).
(15(19:23) sts)

Next row: p1, p2tog three(four:five) times, p1, p2tog
three(four:five) times, p1. (9(11:13) sts)

Next row: (ssk) twice(twice:three times), k1(3:1), (k2tog)
twice(twice:three times). (5(7:7) sts)

Break yarn and follow *Sewing up* instructions on page 6.

Thumb, size 6–12 months only

Place 13 sts from holder onto a 3.25mm (UK 10/
US 3) needle.

With RS facing, using yarn A and 3.25mm (UK 10/US 3)
needles, pick up and knit 1 st from thumb gap before sts on
needles, then knit 13 sts from needle. (14 sts)

Work 3 rows in st st.

Next row: (ssk) three times, k1, (k2tog) three times,
k1. (8 sts)

Next row: (p2tog) to end. (4 sts)

Break yarn, leaving a long tail, and thread through remaining
sts, pull tight and secure. Sew up side of thumb.

Note: Chart position for 2nd mitten

For the second mitten place chart as follows:

Sizes 0–3 and 3–6 months

Row 13: k17(21), work chart, k to end.

Row 14: p2(4), work chart, p to end.

Complete as for first mitten.

Size 6–12 months

Row 15: k to marker, sm, m1, k to marker, m1, sm, k4,
work chart, k to end. (41 sts)

Row 16: p5, work chart, p to marker, sm, p to marker, sm,
p to end.

Complete as for first mitten.

Bird

Materials:

4-ply (fingering) weight yarn
  Yarn A: 1 x 50g (1.75oz) ball, cream
  Yarn B: small amount, yellow
  Yarn C: small amount, grey

2 stitch markers

Stitch holder

Instructions:

Knitted flat.

Make two.

Cast on 26(32:36) sts in yarn B and 2.75mm (UK 12/US 2) needles.

Row 1 (RS): k2(0:0), (p2, k2) to end.

Change to yarn A.

Row 2: (p2, k2) to last 2(0:0) sts, p2(0:0).

Row 3: k2(0:0), (p2, k2) to end.

Repeat rows 2 and 3 three more times, working stripes as follows: 2 rows in yarn C, 2 rows in yarn A, 2 rows in yarn B.

Change to 3mm (UK 11/US 2) needles and yarn A.

Row 10 (WS): p13(16:18), m1, p to end. (27(33:37) sts)

Row 11: k.

Continue in st st for rest of pattern.

Needles:

3 pairs – 2.75mm (UK 12/US 2), 3mm (UK 11/US 2) and 3.25mm (UK 10/US 3) needles

Tapestry (blunt-end) needle for sewing up

Tension:

30 sts x 38 rows = 10cm/4in over st st using 3mm (UK 11/US 2) needles

Sizes 0–3 months and 3–6 months only

Continue in yarn A.

Work 3 rows in st st.

Starting with row 1 of the Bird chart, work as follows:

Row 15: k2(4), work chart, k to end.

Row 16: p15(19), work chart, p to end.

Continue in st st until chart is complete.

Work 1(3) rows in st st in yarn A only, ending with a purl row.

Size 6–12 months only

Continue in yarn A.

Work 3 rows in st st.

Starting with row 1 of the Bird chart, work as follows:

Row 15: k4, work chart, k4, place marker, m1, k1, m1, place marker, k to end. (39 sts)

Chart:

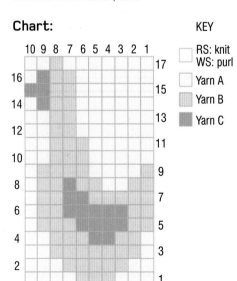

KEY

- RS: knit / WS: purl
- Yarn A
- Yarn B
- Yarn C

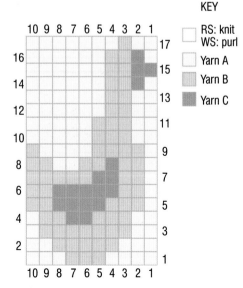

KEY

- RS: knit / WS: purl
- Yarn A
- Yarn B
- Yarn C

Row 16: p to marker, sm, p to marker, sm, p4, work chart, p to end.

Row 17: k4, work chart, k to marker, sm, m1, k to marker, m1, sm, k to end. (41 sts)

Row 18: p to marker, sm, p to marker, sm, p4, work chart, p to end.

Repeat last 2 rows four more times, until there are 13 sts between markers. (49 sts)

Row 27: k4, work chart, k to marker, remove marker, place 13 sts from between markers on holder, cast on 1 st, remove marker, k to end. (37 sts)

Continue in st st until chart is complete.

Work 5 rows in st st in yarn A only, ending with a purl row.

All sizes

Continue in yarn A only.

Next row: k2(3:3), (ssk) twice, k2(4:6), (k2tog) twice, k3(4:4), (ssk) twice, k2(4:3), (k2tog) twice, k2. (19(25:29) sts)

Next row: p.

Next row: k2, ssk(ssk twice:ssk twice), k2(2:4), k2tog(k2tog twice:k2tog twice), k3(2:4), ssk(ssk twice:ssk twice), k2(2:4), k2tog(k2tog twice:k2tog twice), k1. (15(17:21) sts)

Next row: p1, p2tog three(three:four) times, p1(3:3), p2tog three(three:four) times, p1. (9(11:13) sts)

Break yarn and follow *Sewing up* instructions on page 6.

Thumb, size 6–12 months only

Place 13 sts from holder onto a 3.25mm (UK 10/US 3) needle.

With RS facing, using yarn A and 3.25mm (UK 10/US 3) needles, pick up and knit 1 st from thumb gap before sts on needles, then knit 13 sts from needle. (14 sts)

Work 3 rows in st st.

Next row: k1, (ssk) three times, (k2tog) three times, k1. (8 sts)

Next row: (p2tog) twice, p1, (p2tog) twice. (4 sts)

Break yarn, leaving a long tail, and thread through remaining sts, pull tight and secure. Sew up side of thumb.

Note: Chart position for 2nd mitten

For the second mitten place chart as follows:

Sizes 0–3 and 3–6 months

Row 15: k15(19), work chart, k to end.

Row 16: p2(4), work chart, p to end.

Complete as for first mitten.

Size 6–12 months

Row 15: k to marker, sm, m1, k to marker, m1, sm, k4, work chart k to end. (41 sts)

Row 16: p5, work chart, p to marker, sm, p to marker, sm, p to end.

Complete as for first mitten.

Embroidery

Using the photo for guidance, embroider the legs using yarn C and chain stitch and embroider the eyes using yarn A and a French knot (see page 6 for stitch instructions).

Embroidered Flowers

Materials:

4-ply (fingering) weight yarn
 Yarn A: 1 x 50g (1.75oz) ball, cream
 Yarn B: small amount, pink
 Yarn C: small amount, amber

2 stitch markers

Stitch holder

Needles:

2 pairs – 3mm (UK 11/US 2) and 3.25mm (UK 10/ US 3) needles

Tapestry (blunt-end) needle for sewing up

Tension:

28 sts x 36 rows = 10cm/4in, over st st using 3.25mm (UK 10/US 3) needles

Instructions:

Knitted flat.

Make two.

Cast on 27(33:37) sts using yarn A and 3mm (UK 11/ US 2) needles.

Rows 1–10: k.

Change to 3.25mm (UK 10/US 3) needles.

Row 11 (RS): k.

Row 12: p.

Row 13: k2(3:4), *ssk, yo, k2(3:3), repeat from * to last 5(5:8) sts, ssk, yo, k3(4:6).

Row 14: p.

Continue in st st for rest of pattern.

Sizes 0–3 months and 3–6 months only

Continue in st st until mitten measures 9(9.5)cm/3½(3¾)in from cast-on edge, ending with a purl row.

Size 6–12 months only

Row 15: k18, place marker, m1, k1, m1, place marker, k to end. (39 sts)

Row 16: p to marker, sm, p to marker, p to end.

Row 17: k to marker, sm, m1, k to marker, m1, sm, k to end. (41 sts)

Row 18: p to marker, sm, p to marker, sm, p to end.

Repeat last 2 rows four more times. (49 sts)

Row 27: k to marker, remove marker, place 13 sts from between markers on holder, remove marker, cast on 1 st, k to end. (37 sts)

Continue in st st until mitten measures 10.5cm/4⅛in from cast-on edge, ending with a purl row.

All sizes

Next row: k2(3:3), (ssk) twice, k2(4:6), (k2tog) twice, k3, (ssk) twice, k2(4:6), (k2tog) twice, k2(3:3). (19(25:29) sts)

Next row: p.

Next row: k2, ssk(ssk twice:ssk twice), k2(2:4), k2tog(k2tog twice:k2tog twice), k3(1:1), ssk(ssk twice:ssk twice), k2(2:4), k2tog(k2tog twice:k2tog twice), k2. (15(17:21) sts)

Next row: p1, (p2tog) three(three:four) times, p1(3:3), (p2tog) three(three:four) times, p1. (9(11:13) sts)

Next row: (ssk) twice(twice:three) times, k1(3:1), (k2tog) twice(twice:three) times. (5(5:7) sts)

Break yarn and follow *Sewing up* instructions on page 6.

Thumb, size 6–12 months only

Place 13 sts from holder onto a 3.25mm (UK 10/ US 3) needle.

With RS facing, using yarn A and 3.25mm (UK 10/US 3) needles, pick up and knit 1 st from thumb gap before sts on needles, then knit 13 sts from needle. (14 sts)

Work 3 rows in st st.

Next row: k1, (ssk) three times, k1, (k2tog) three times, k1. (8 sts)

Next row: (p2tog) to end. (4 sts)

Break yarn, leaving a long tail, and thread through remaining sts, pull tight and secure. Sew up side of thumb.

Embroidery

Using the photo for guidance and yarns B and C, embroider flowers as follows:

Embroider petals using yarn B and lazy daisy stitch (see page 6), making five petals per flower. Embroider the centre of the flowers with a French knot (see page 6) using yarn C.

Tie

Make two.

Cut six strands of yarn C 50cm/20in long. Plait to form a tie and thread through the holes.

Frog

Materials:

Baby – between 4-ply (fingering) and DK (US sport) weight yarn
  Yarn A: 1 x 50g (1.75oz) ball, lime
  Yarn B: small amount, cream

2 stitch markers

Stitch holder

Needles:

2 pairs – 3mm (UK 11/US 2) and 3.25mm (UK 10/US 3) needles

Tapestry (blunt-end) needle for sewing up

Tension:

25 sts x 34 rows = 10cm/4in, over st st using 3.25mm (UK 10/US 3) needles

Instructions:

Knitted flat.

Make two.

Cast on 24(28:32) sts using yarn B and 3mm (UK 11/US 2) needles.

Change to yarn A.

Row 1: (k2, p2) to end.

Row 2: (p2, k2) to end.

Repeat rows 1 and 2 three(three:four) more times.

Change to 3.25mm (UK 10/US 3) needles.

Next row (RS): k.

Next row: p.

Continue in st st throughout rest of pattern.

Sizes 0–3 months and 3–6 months only

Continue in st st until mitten measures 9(9.5)cm/3½(3¾)in from cast-on edge, ending with a purl row.

Size 6–12 months only

Work 2 rows in st st.

Row 13: k16, place marker, m1, place marker, k to end. (33 sts)

Row 14: p to end, slipping markers.

Row 15: k to marker, sm, m1, k to marker, m1, sm, k to end. (35 sts)

Row 16: p to end, slipping markers.

Repeat last 2 rows four more times, until there are 11 sts between the markers. (43 sts)

Next row: k to marker, remove marker, place 11 sts from between markers on holder, cast on 1 st, remove marker, k to end. (32 sts)

Continue in st st until mitten measures 13cm/5in from cast-on edge, ending with purl row.

All sizes

Next row: k1(3:1), (ssk) twice, k2(2:4), (k2tog) twice, k2(2:4), (ssk) twice, k2(2:4), (k2tog) twice, k1(3:1). (16(20:24) sts)

Next row: p.

Next row: k0(1:1), (ssk) twice, k0(0:2), (k2tog) twice, k0(2:2), (ssk) twice, k0(0:2), (k2tog) twice, k0(1:1). (8(12:16) sts

Next row: (p2tog) to end. (4(6:8) sts)

Sizes 0–3 months and 3–6 months only

Next row: (p2tog) to end. (6(8) sts)

All sizes

Break yarn and follow *Sewing up* instructions on page 6.

Thumb, size 6–12 months only

Place 11 sts from holder onto a 3.25mm (UK 10/US 3) needle.

With RS facing, using yarn A and 3.25mm (UK 10/US 3) needles, pick up and knit 1 st from thumb gap before sts on needles; knit 11 sts from needle, pick up and knit 1 st from gap. (13 sts)

Work 3 rows in st st.

Next row: (ssk) three times, k1, (k2tog) three times. (7 sts)

Break yarn, leaving a long tail, and thread through remaining sts, pull tight and secure. Sew up side of thumb.

Eye pads

Make eight.

Cast on 5 sts using yarn A and 3.25mm (UK 10/US 3) needles.

Row 1: k.

Row 2: p.

Rows 3 and 4: Repeat rows 1 and 2.

Row 5: k2tog, k1, k2tog. (3 sts)

Cast off remaining 3 sts.

Eye spots
Make four.
Cast on 1 st using yarn B and 3mm (UK 11/US 2) needles.

Row 1: kfb. (2 sts)

Row 2: p

Row 3: k1, m1, k1. (3 sts)

Row 4: p.

Row 5: k1, k2tog. (2 sts)

Row 6: p2tog and fasten off.

Embroidery
Using the photo for guidance and yarn B, embroider the mouth using chain stitch (see page 6), making sure you have one right and one left mitten.

To make up, all sizes
Using the photo for guidance and yarn B, attach one eye spot to one eye pad. With WS together, sew this eye pad to another eye pad without the eye spot. Repeat for other eyes.

Weave in ends. Use long tail of yarn to sew up side seam of mitten. Attach eyes.

Fair Isle Border

Materials:

Baby – between 4-ply (fingering) and DK (US sport) weight yarn
Yarn A: 1 x 50g (1.75oz) ball, colour, red
Yarn B: small amount, cream
Yarn C: small amount, lime

2 stitch markers

Stitch holder

Needles:

Set of 2.75mm (UK 12/US 2) DPN, or a 2.75mm (UK 12/US 2) circular needle

Tapestry (blunt-end) needle for sewing up

Tension:

26 sts x 34 rounds = 10cm/4in, over st st using 3mm (UK 11/US 2) needles

Chart:

KEY

☐	RS: knit WS:purl
■	Yarn A
▨	Yarn B
▨	Yarn C

Instructions:

These mittens are worked in the round using either double-pointed needles, or a circular needle and the magic loop method.

Make two.

Cast on 24(30:36) sts with yarn A and 2.75mm (UK 12/US 2) DPN or a 2.75mm (UK 12/US 2) circular needle, then join in the round, taking care not to twist stitches.

Round 1: (k1, p1) repeat to end.

Repeat round 1 five(five:seven) more times.

Next round: k.

Starting with round 1, work the 4 rounds of the Fair Isle Border chart as set, repeating the 6 st pattern four(five:six) times per round.

Sizes 0–3 months and 3–6 months only

Continue in st st (k all rounds) using yarn A until mitten measures 9(10)cm/3½(4)in from cast-on edge.

Continue in st st and yarn A for rest of mitten.

Size 6–12 months only

Next round: k17, k2tog, k to end in yarn A. (35 sts)

Continue in st st and yarn A for rest of mitten.

Work 1 round.

Next round: k17, place marker, m1, k1, m1, place marker, k to end. (37 sts)

Next round: k to end, slipping markers.

Next round: k to marker, sm, m1, k to marker, m1, sm, k to end. (39 sts)

Repeat last 2 rounds four more times, until there are 13 sts between markers. (47 sts)

Next round: k to marker, remove marker, place 13 sts from between markers on holder, k to end. (34 sts)

Continue in st st until mitten measures 11cm/4¼in from cast-on edge.

All sizes

Next round: (k2tog, k2) to last 0(2:2) st(s), k0(k2tog:k2tog). (18(22:25) sts)

Next round: k.

Next round: (k1, k2tog) to last 0(1:1) st, k0(1:1). (12(15:17) sts)

Next round: (k2tog) to end to last 0(1:1) st, k0(1:1). (6(8:9) sts)

Break yarn and follow *Sewing up* instructions on page 6.

Thumb, size 6–12 months only

Place 13 sts from holder onto a 2.75mm (UK 12/US 2) DPN or a 2.75mm (UK 12/US 2) circular needle.

With RS facing, using yarn A, pick up and knit 1 st from thumb gap before sts on needle/s, then knit 13 sts from needle and arrange in the round. (14 sts)

Work 3 rounds.

Next row: (ssk) three times, (k2tog) four times. (7 sts)

Break yarn and thread through remaining sts, pull tight and secure. Weave in ends.

Heart

Materials:

Baby – between 4-ply (fingering) and DK (US sport) weight yarn
  Yarn A: 1 x 50g (1.75oz) ball, cream
  Yarn B: small amount, pink

2 stitch markers

Stitch holder

Needles:

2 pairs – 3mm (UK 11/US 2) and 3.25mm (UK 10/ US 3) needles

Tapestry (blunt-end) needle for sewing up

Tension:

25 sts x 34 rows = 10cm/4in over st st using 3.25mm (UK 10/US 3) needles

Chart:

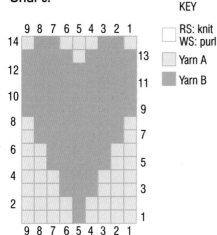

KEY

☐ RS: knit
  WS: purl
▨ Yarn A
▨ Yarn B

Row 13: k2(3), work chart, k to end.

Row 14: p14(17) work chart, p to end.

Continue in st st until all chart rows are complete.

Work 2(4) rows in st st using yarn A, ending with a purl row.

Size 6–12 months only

Continue in st st and yarn A.

Row 11: k16, place marker, m1, k1, m1, place marker, k to end. (35 sts)

Row 12: p to marker, sm, p to marker, p to end.***

Starting with row 1 of the Heart chart, work as follows:

Row 13: k4, work chart, k to marker, sm, m1, k to marker, m1, sm, k to end. (37 sts)

Row 14: p to marker, sm, p to marker, sm, p3, work chart, p to end.

Repeat last 2 rows three more times, until there are 11 sts between brackets. (43 sts)

Row 21: k4, work chart, k to marker, remove marker, place 11 sts from between markers on holder, cast on 1 st, remove marker, k to end. (33 sts)

Continue in st st until chart is complete.

Work 6 rows in st st using yarn A, ending with a purl row.

All sizes

Continue in st st and yarn A.

Next row: k2(2:3), (ssk) twice, k1(3:3), (k2tog) twice, k1(1:2), k1, k2(2:3), (ssk) twice, k1(3:3), (k2tog twice, k1(1:2). (17(21:25) sts)

Next row: p.

Next row: k2, ssk(ssk:ssk twice), k1(3:1), k2tog(k2tog:k2tog twice), k3, ssk(ssk:ssk twice), k1(3:1), k2tog(k2tog:k2tog twice), k2. (13(17:17) sts)

Next row: (p2tog) three(four:four) times, p1, (p2tog) three(four:four) times. (7(9:9) sts)

Break yarn and follow *Sewing up* instructions on page 6.

Instructions:

Knitted flat.

Right mitten

Cast on 25(29:33) sts using yarn A and 3mm (UK 10/ US 2) needles.

Row 1 (RS): k1, (p1, k1) to end.

Row 2: p1, (k1, p1) to end.

Repeat rows 1 and 2 twice more.

Change to 3.25mm (UK 10/US 3) needles.

Row 7 (RS): k.

Row 8: p.

Row 9: k1, (yo, k2tog) to end.

Row 10: p.

Continue in st st for rest of mitten.

Sizes 0–3 months and 3–6 months only

Work 2 rows in st st using yarn A.**

Starting with row 1 of the Heart chart, work as follows:

Thumb, size 6–12 months only

Place 11 sts from holder onto a 3.25mm (UK 10/US 3) needle.

With RS facing, using yarn A and 3.25mm (UK 10/US 3) needles, pick up and knit 1 st from thumb gap before sts on needles; knit 11 sts from needle, pick up and knit 1 st from gap. (13 sts)

Work 3 rows in st st.

Next row: (ssk) three times, k1, (k2tog) three times. (7 sts)

Break yarn, leaving a long tail, and thread through remaining sts, pull tight and secure. Sew up side of thumb.

Left mitten

Sizes 0–3 months and 3–6 months only

Work as right mitten to **.

Starting with row 1 of the Heart chart, continue in st st as follows:

Row 13: k14(17), work chart, k to end.

Row 14: p2(3), work chart, p to end.

Complete as for right mitten, keeping chart correct.

Size 6–12 months only

Work as right mitten to ***.

Starting with row 1 of the Heart chart, continue in st st as follows:

Row 13: k to marker, sm, m1, k to marker, m1, sm, k3, work chart, k to end.

Row 14: p4, work chart, p to marker, sm, p to marker, sm, p to end.

These two rows set the position for the chart and thumb shaping. Complete as for right mitten, keeping chart correct.

To make up all sizes

Weave in ends. Use long tail of yarn to sew up side seam of mitten.

Tie
Make two.

Cut six strands of yarn B 50cm/20in long. Plait to form a tie and thread through holes above rib pattern.

Ladybird

Materials:

4-ply (fingering) weight yarn
  Yarn A: 1 x 50g (1.75oz) ball, cream
  Yarn B: small amount, red
  Yarn C: small amount, black

2 stitch markers

Stitch holder

Chart:

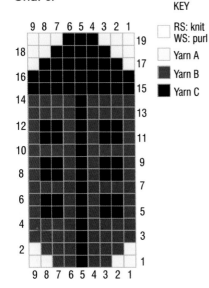

KEY
☐ RS: knit WS: purl
☐ Yarn A
▨ Yarn B
■ Yarn C

Instructions:

Knitted flat.

Make two.

Cast on 26(32:36) sts using yarn C and 3mm (UK 11/US 2) needles.

Change to yarn B.

Row 1: k2(0:0), (p2, k2) to end.

Row 2: (p2, k2) to last 2(0:0) sts, p2(0:0).

Repeat rows 1 and 2 three(three:four) more times.

Change to 3.25mm (UK 10/US 3) needles and yarn A.

Next row (RS): k13(16:18), m1, k to end. (27(33:37) sts)

Next row: p.

Sizes 0–3 months and 3–6 months only

Starting with row 1 of the Ladybird chart, work as follows:

Row 11: k3(5), work chart, k to end.

Needles:

2 pairs – 3mm (UK 11/US 2) and 3.25mm (UK 10/US 3) needles

Tapestry (blunt-end) needle for sewing up

Tension:

28 sts x 34 rows = 10cm/4in over st st using 3.25mm (UK 10/US 3) needles

Row 12: p15(19), work chart, p to end.

Continue in st st until chart is complete.

Continue in yarn A and st st for 1(3) row(s), ending with a purl row.

Size 6–12 months only

Continue in yarn A.

Work 2 rows in st st.

Row 15: k18, place marker, m1, k1, m1, place marker, k to end. (39 sts)

Row 16: p to marker, sm, p to marker, sm, p to end.

Starting with row 1 of the Ladybird chart, work as follows:

Row 17: k5, work chart, k to marker, sm, m1, k to marker, m1, sm, k to end. (41 sts)

Row 18: p to marker, sm, p to marker, sm, p4, work chart, p to end.

Repeat last 2 rows four more times, until there are 13 sts between markers. (49 sts)

Next row: k5, work chart, k to marker, remove marker, place 13 sts from between markers on holder, cast on 1 st, remove marker, k to end. (37 sts)

Work 3 rows in yarn A only, ending with a purl row.

All sizes

Continue in yarn A only.

Next row: k2(3:3), (ssk) twice, k2(4:6), (k2tog) twice, k3, (ssk) twice, k2(4:6), (k2tog) twice, k2(3:3). (19(25:29) sts)

Next row: p.

Next row: k2, ssk(ssk twice:ssk twice), k2(2:4), k2tog(k2tog twice:k2tog twice), k3(1:1), ssk(ssk twice:ssk twice), k2(2:4), k2tog(k2tog twice:k2tog twice), k2. (15(17:21) sts)

Next row: p1, (p2tog) three(three:four) times, p1(3:3), (p2tog) three(three:four) times, p1. (9(11:13) sts)

Next row: (ssk) twice(twice:three times), k1(3:1), (k2tog) twice(twice:three times). (5(7:7) sts)

Break yarn and follow *Sewing up* instructions on page 6.

Thumb, size 6–12 months only

Place 13 sts from holder onto a 3.25mm (UK 10/US 3) needle.

With RS facing, using yarn A and 3.25mm (UK 10/US 3) needles, pick up and knit 1 st from thumb gap before sts on needles, then knit 13 sts from needle. (14 sts)

Work 3 rows in st st.

Next row: (ssk) three times, k1, (k2tog) three times, k1. (8 sts)

Next row: (p2tog to end). (4 sts)

Break yarn, leaving a long tail, and thread through remaining sts, pull tight and secure. Sew up side of thumb.

Note: Chart position for 2nd mitten

For the second mitten place chart as follows:

Sizes 0–3 and 3–6 months

Row 11: k15(19), work chart, k to end.

Row 12: P3(5), work chart, p to end.

Complete as for first mitten from end of row 12.

Size 6–12 months

Row 15: k to marker, sm, m1, k to marker, m1, sm, k4, work chart k to end. (41 sts)

Row 16: p5, work chart, p to marker, sm, p to marker, sm, p to end.

Complete as for first mitten from row 17, keeping chart placement correct.

To make up all sizes

Weave in ends. Use long tail of yarn to sew up side seam of mitten.

Embroidery

With the photo as a guide, embroider legs and antennae stalk in yarn C, using chain stitch for the legs and French knots for the ends of the antennae (see page 6 for stitch instructions). Using yarn A, embroider the eyes using French knots.

Dashes

Materials:
4-ply (fingering) weight yarn
   1 x 50g (1.75oz) ball, aqua
2 stitch markers
Stitch holder

Needles:
2 pairs – 3mm (UK 11/US 2) and 3.25mm (UK 10/US 3) needles
Tapestry (blunt-end) needle for sewing up

Tension:
28 sts x 36 rows = 10cm/4in over st st using 3.25mm (UK 10/US 3) needles

Dash pattern:
Row 1 (RS): p4, (k1tbl, p5) repeat to last 4 sts, k1tbl, p3.

Row 2: k4, (p1tbl, k5) repeat to last 4 sts, p1tbl, k3.

Rows 3–6: repeat rows 1 and 2 twice more.

Row 7: p1, (k1tbl, p5) repeat to last st, p1.

Row 8: k1, (k5, p1tbl) repeat to last st k1.

Rows 9–12: repeat rows 7 and 8 twice more.

Instructions:
Knitted flat.

Make two.

Cast on 26(32:38) sts using aqua yarn and 3mm (UK 11/US 2) needles.

Row 1 (RS): k2(3:2), (p2, k2) to last 0(1:0) st, k1(1:0).

Row 2: p3(3:2), (k2, p2) to last 1(1:0) st, p1(1:0).

Repeat rows 1 and 2 three(three:four) more times.

Change to 3.25mm (UK 10/US 3) needles and work in dash pattern.

Sizes 0–3 months and 3–6 months only
Continue in dash pattern until mitten measures 9(9.5cm/3½(3¾)in from cast-on edge, ending with row 6 or row 12 of dash pattern.

Size 6–12 months only
Work 4 rows in dash pattern.

Next row (RS): patt 19, place marker, m1, place marker, patt to end. (39 sts)

Next row: patt 19, sm, k1, sm, patt to end.

Next row: patt to marker, sm, m1, p to marker, m1, sm, patt to end. (41 sts)

Next row: patt to marker, sm, k to marker, sm, patt to end.

Repeat last 2 rows five more times, until there are 13 sts between markers. (51 sts)

Next row (RS): patt to marker, remove marker, place 13 sts from between markers on holder, remove marker, patt to end. (38 sts)

Continue in dash pattern until mitten measures 0.5cm/4⅛in from cast-on edge, ending with row 6 or row 12 of dash pattern.

All sizes
Continue in rev st st only.

Next row: p2(3:2), (p2tog) twice(twice:three times), p2(3:3), (p2tog) twice(twice:three times), p2(4:4), (p2tog) twice(twice:three times), p2(3:3), (p2tog) twice(twice:three times), p2(3:2). (18(24:26) sts)

Next row: k.

Next row: p1(1:2), (p2tog) twice, p0(1:1), (p2tog) twice, p2(2:4), (p2tog) twice, p0(1:1), (p2tog) twice, p1(1:2). (10(16:18) sts)

Next row: (k2tog) to end. (5(8:9) sts)

Break yarn and follow *Sewing up* instructions on page 6.

Thumb, size 6–12 months only
Place 13 sts from holder onto a 3.25mm (UK 10/US 2) needle.

With RS facing, using yarn A and 3.25mm (UK 10/US 2) needles, pick up and purl 1 st from thumb gap before sts on needles, then purl 13 sts from needle. (14 sts)

Work 4 rows in rev st st.

Next row (WS): (ssk) three times, k1, (k2tog) three times, k1. (8 sts)

Next row: (p2tog) to end. (4 sts)

Break yarn, leaving a long tail, and thread through remaining sts, pull tight and secure. Sew up side of thumb.

Mouse

Materials:

Baby – between 4-ply (fingering) and DK (US sport)
weight yarn
  Yarn A: 1 x 50g (1.75oz) ball, beige
  Yarn B: small amount, cream
  Yarn C: small amount, pink

2 stitch markers

Stitch holder

Needles:

2 pairs – 3mm (UK 11/US 2) and 3.25mm (UK 10/
US 3) needles

Tapestry (blunt-end) needle for sewing up

Tension:

25 sts x 34 rows = 10cm/4in over st st using 3.25mm
(UK 10/US 3) needles

Instructions:

Knitted flat.

Make two.

Cast on 24(28:32) sts using yarn B and 3mm (UK 11/
US 2) needles.

Change to yarn A.

Row 1: (k2, p2) to end.

Row 2: (k2, p2) to end.

Repeat rows 1 and 2 three(three:four) more times.

Change to 3.25mm (UK 10/US 3) needles.

Next row: k.

Next row: p.

Continue in st st for rest of mitten.

Sizes 0–3 months and 3–6 months only

Continue in st st until mitten measures 9(9.5)cm/3½(3¾)in
from cast-on edge, ending with a purl row.

Size 6–12 months only

Work 2 rows in st st.

Row 13: k16, place marker, m1, place marker, k to end.
(33 sts)

Row 14: p to end, slipping markers.

Row 15: k to marker, sm, m1, k to marker, m1, sm,
k to end. (35 sts)

Row 16: p to end, slipping markers.

Repeat last 2 rows four more times, until there are 11 sts
between the markers. (43 sts)

Next row: k to marker, remove marker, place 11 sts from
between markers on holder, cast on 1 st, remover marker, k
to end. (32 sts)

Continue in st st until mitten measures 11cm/4¼in from
cast-on edge, ending with a purl row.

All sizes

Next row: k1(3:2), (ssk) twice, k2(2:4), (k2tog) twice,
k2(2:4), (ssk) twice, k2(2:4), (k2tog) twice, k1(3:2).
(16(20:24) sts)

Next row: p.

Next row: k0(1:1), (ssk) twice, k0(0:2), (k2tog) twice,
k0(2:2), (ssk) twice, k0(0:2), (k2tog) twice, k0(1:1).
(8(12:16) sts)

Sizes 3–6 months and 6–12 months only

Next row: (p2tog) to end. (6(8) sts)

All sizes

Break yarn and follow *Sewing up* instructions on page 6.

Thumb, size 6–12 months only

Place 11 sts from holder onto a 3.25mm (UK 10/
US 3) needle.

With RS facing, using yarn A and 3.25mm (UK 10/US 3)
needles, pick up and knit 1 st from thumb gap before sts on
needles; knit 11 sts from needle, pick up and knit 1 st from
gap. (13 sts)

Work 3 rows in st st.

Next row: (ssk) three times, k1, (k2tog) three times. (7 sts)

Break yarn, leaving a long tail, and thread through remaining
sts, pull tight and secure. Sew up side of thumb.

Ears

Make eight.

Cast on 5 sts, using yarn C and 3.25mm (UK 10/
US 3) needles.

Row 1 (WS): p.

Row 2: k.

Row 3: p.

Row 4: k.

Row 5: p.

Row 6: ssk, k1, k2tog. (3 sts)

Row 7: p.

Cast off.

Embroidery

Using the photo for guidance, embroider eyes and nose with French knots using yarn C and embroider whiskers in chain stitch using yarn B, making sure you have one right and one left mitten (see page 6 for stitch instructions).

To make up all sizes

With wrong sides together and yarn C, sew two ear pieces together. Repeat for other ears.

Weave in ends. Use long tail of yarn to sew up side seam of mitten. Attach ears.

Little Star

Materials:

Baby – between 4-ply (fingering) and DK (US sport) weight yarn
  Yarn A: small amount, lime
  Yarn B: 1 x 50g (1.75oz) ball, cream
  Yarn C: small amount, aqua

2 stitch markers

Stitch holder

Chart:

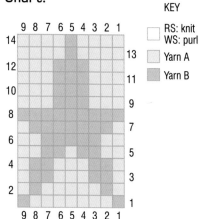

KEY

☐ RS: knit
  WS: purl

▨ Yarn A

▨ Yarn B

Instructions:

Knitted flat.

Make two.

Cast on 27(31:35) sts using yarn A and 3mm (UK 10/US 2) needles.

Change to yarn B.

Row 1: k1, (p1, k1) to end.

Row 2: p1, (k1, p1) to end.

Repeat last 2 rows three more times, working stripes as follows: 2 rows in yarn C, 2 rows in yarn B, 2 rows in yarn A.

Change to 3.25mm (UK 10/US 3) needles and yarn B.

Row 9 (RS): k.

Row 10: p.

Continue in st st for rest of pattern.

Sizes 0–3 months and 3–6 months only

Continue in yarn B.

Work 4 rows in st st.

Starting with row 1 of Little Star chart, work as follows:

Needles:

2 pairs – 3mm (UK 11/US 2) and 3.25mm (UK 10/US 3) needles

Tapestry (blunt-end) needle for sewing up

Tension:

25 sts x 34 rows = 10cm/4in over st st using 3.25mm (UK 10/US 3) needles

Row 15: k3(k4), work chart, k to end.

Row 16: p15(18), work chart, p to end.

Continue in st st until all chart rows are complete.

Work 2(4) rows in st st using yarn B only.

Size 6–12 months only

Continue in yarn B.

Work 2 rows in st st.

Row 13: k17, place marker, m1, k1, m1, place marker, k to end. (37 sts)

Row 14: p to marker, sm, p to marker, sm, p to end.

Starting with row 1 of Little Star chart, work as follows:

Row 15: k5, work chart, k to marker, sm, m1, k to marker, m1, sm, k to end. (39 sts)

Row 16: p to marker, sm, p to marker, sm, p3, work chart, p to end.

Repeat last 2 rows three more times, until there are 11 sts between markers. (45 sts)

Next row: k5, work chart, k to marker, remove marker, place 11 sts from between markers on holder, cast on 1 st, remove marker, k to end. (35 sts)

Continue in st st until chart is complete.

Work 6 rows in st st using yarn B only.

All sizes

Continue in yarn B only.

Next row: k1, (ssk) twice(three times:three times), k3(1:3), (k2tog) twice(three times:three times), k3, (ssk) twice(three times:three times), k3(1:3), (k2tog) twice(three times:three times), k1. (19(19:23) sts)

Next row: p.

Next row: k0(0:1), (ssk) twice, k1, (k2tog) twice, k1(1:3), (ssk) twice, k1, (k2tog) twice, k0(0:1). (11(11:15) sts)

Next row: p1, (p2tog) twice(twice:three times), p1, (p2tog) twice(twice:three times), p1. (7(7:9) sts)

Break yarn and follow *Sewing up* instructions on page 6.

Thumb, size 6–12 months only

Place 11 sts from holder onto a 3.25mm (UK 10/US 3) needle.

With RS facing, using yarn B and 3.25mm (UK 10/US 3) needles, pick up and knit 1 st from thumb gap before sts on needles; knit 11 sts from needle, pick up and knit 1 st from gap. (13 sts)

Work 3 rows in st st.

Next row: (ssk) three times, k1, (k2tog) three times. (7 sts)

Break yarn, leaving a long tail, and thread through remaining sts, pull tight and secure. Sew up side of thumb.

Note: Chart position for 2nd mitten

For the second mitten place chart as follows:

Sizes 0–3 and 3–6 months

Row 15: k15(18), work chart, k to end.

Row 16: p3(4), work chart, p to end.

Complete as for first mitten.

Size 6–12 months

Row 15: k to marker, sm, m1, k to marker, m1, sm, k4, work chart k to end. (41 sts)

Row 16: p5, p, work chart, p to marker, sm, p to marker, sm, p to end.

Complete as for first mitten.

Owl

Materials:

Baby – between 4-ply (fingering) and DK (US sport) weight yarn
Yarn A: 1 x 50g (1.75oz) ball, camel
Yarn B: small amount, chocolate
Yarn C: small amount, cream
Yarn D: small amount, coral

2 stitch markers

Stitch holder

Fleck pattern:

Round 1 (RS): k using yarn A.

Round 2: (k1 in yarn A, k1 in yarn B, k2 in yarn A) to end.

Round 3: k using yarn A.

Round 4: (k3 in yarn A, k1 in yarn B) to end.

Instructions:

These mittens are worked in the round using either double-pointed needles, or a circular needle and the magic loop method.

Make two.

Cast on 24(28:32) sts in yarn A using 3mm (UK 11/US 2) DPN or a 3mm (UK 11/US 2) circular needle, then join in the round, taking care not to twist stitches.

Round 1: p.

Round 2: k.

Repeat rounds 1 and 2 twice(twice:three times) more.

Change to 3.25mm (UK 10/US 3) needle/s.

Next round: *k2, yo, k2tog, k2(3:2), yo, k2tog*, repeat * to * to last 0(1:0) st, k0(1:0).

Sizes 0–3 months and 3–6 months only

Work 12(14) rounds in fleck pattern.

Continue in yarn A only, until mitten measures 9(10)cm/3½(4)in from cast-on edge.

Size 6–12 months only

Work 2 rounds in fleck pattern.

Continue in fleck pattern as follows:

Round 13: patt 16, place marker, m1, place marker, patt to end. (33 sts)

Round 14: patt to end, slipping markers and working sts between markers in yarn A only.

Round 15: patt to marker, sm, m1, k to marker in yarn A, m1, sm, patt to end. (35 sts)

Needles:

2 sets – 3mm (UK 11/US 2) and 3.25mm (UK 10/US 3) DPN, or 3mm (UK 11/US 2) and 3.25mm (UK 10/US 3) circular needles

Tapestry (blunt-end) needle for sewing up

Tension:

25 sts x 34 rounds = 10cm (4in), in st st using 3.25mm (UK 10/US 3) needles

Round 16: patt to end, slipping markers and working sts between markers in yarn A only.

Repeat last 2 rounds four more times, until there are 11 sts between markers. (43 sts)

Next round: patt to marker, keeping patt correct; remove marker, place 11 sts from between markers on holder, remove marker, patt to end. (32 sts)

Continue in yarn A only, until mitten measures 10.5cm/4⅛in from cast-on edge.

All sizes

Continue in yarn A only.

Next round: (k2, k2tog) to end. 18(21:24) sts.

Next round: k.

Next round: (k1, k2tog) to end. 12(14:16) sts.

Next round: k2tog to end. (6(7:8) sts)

Break yarn and follow *Sewing up* instructions on page 6.

Thumb, size 6–12 months only

Place 11 sts from holder onto 3.25mm (UK 10/US 3) DPN or a 3.25mm (UK 10/US 3) circular needle.

With RS facing, using yarn A, pick up and knit 1 st from thumb gap before sts on needle/s; knit 11 sts from needle, pick up and knit 1 st from gap. (13 sts)

Work 3 rounds in st st.

Next round: (ssk) three times, k1, (k2tog) three times. (7 sts)

Break yarn, leaving a long tail, and thread through remaining sts, pull tight and secure. Sew up side of thumb.

Ears

Make four.

Cast on 12 sts, using yarn A and 3mm(3mm:3.25mm) (UK 11/US 2:UK 11/US 2:UK 10/US 3) needle/s.

Row 1: k.

Row 2: p.

Row 3: k1, (ssk, k1, k2tog) twice, k1. (8 sts)

Row 4: p.

Row 5: k1, (sl2 knitwise, k1, p2sso) twice, k1. (4 sts)

Row 6: p1, p2tog, p1. (3 sts)

Break yarn, leaving a long tail, and thread through remaining 3 sts. Fold ear into triangle, and sew up side seam. Repeat for other ears.

Eyes
Make four.

Cast on 2 sts, using yarn C and 3mm(3mm:3.25mm) (UK 11/US 2: UK 11/US 2:UK 10/US 3) needle/s.

Row 1 (WS): p.

Row 2: (kfb) twice. (4 sts)

Row 3: p.

Row 4: k2, m1, k2. (5 sts)

Row 5: p.

Row 6: k2, k2tog, k1. (4 sts)

Row 7: p.

Row 8: ssk, k2tog. (2 sts)

Cast off remaining 2 sts.

Beak
Make four.

Cast on 11 sts, using yarn D and 3mm(3mm:3.25mm) (UK 11/US 2: UK 11/US 2:UK 10/US 3) needle/s, and knit flat.

Row 1: p.

Row 2: k2, ssk, k3, k2tog, k2. (9 sts)

Row 3: p.

Row 4: k2, ssk, k1, k2tog, k2. (7 sts)

Row 5: p2, p3tog, p2. (5 sts)

Row 6: k1, sl2 knitwise, k1, p2sso, k1. (3 sts)

Break yarn, leaving a long tail, and thread through remaining sts. Fold beak in half to make a triangle and sew up side seam.

To make up all sizes

Weave in ends. Using the photo for guidance and matching yarn, attach eyes, beaks and ears, making sure you have one left and one right mitten. Use yarn D and a French knot (see page 6) to embroider the centre of each eye.

Tie
Make two.

Cut six strands of yarn D, 50cm/20in long. Plait to form a tie and thread through top of the border.

Little Twists

Materials:

Baby – between 4-ply (fingering) and DK (US sport) weight yarn, 1 x 50g (1.75oz) ball, camel

2 stitch markers

Stitch holder

Needles:

Pair of 3mm (UK 11/US 2) needles

Cable needle

Tapestry (blunt-end) needle for sewing up

Tension:

26 sts x 33 rows = 10cm/4in over st st using 3mm (UK 11/US 2) needles

Additional abbreviations:

C2B – place 1 st on cable needle and hold to back, k1, k1 from cable needle

C4B – place 2 sts on cable needle and hold to back, k2, k2 from cable needle

Instructions:

Knitted flat.

Make two.

Cast on 29(37:43) sts using camel yarn and 3mm (UK 11/US 2) needles.

Row 1: (k1, p1) to last st, k1.

Row 2: (p1, k1) to last st, p1.

Repeat rows 1 and 2 twice more. (Inc 1 st at centre of 6 sts, 3–6 months only.) (29(38:43) sts)

Sizes 0–3 months and 3–6 months only

Row 7: p2, *k4, p3(2), repeat from * three(five) times, k4, p2.

Row 8: k2, *p4, k3(2), repeat from * three(five) times, p4, k2.

Row 9: p2, *C4B, p3(2), repeat from * three(five) times, C4B, p2.

Row 10: k2, *p4, k3(2), repeat from * three(five) times, p4, k2.

Repeat rows 7–10 until mitten measures 9(10)cm/3½(4)in from cast-on edge, ending on row 10.

Size 6–12 months only

Row 7: p2, (k4, p3) five times, k4, p2.

Row 8: k2, (p4, k3) five times, p4, k2.

These two rows set cable position.

Continue in cable pattern, working thumb increases as follows:

Row 9: p2, (C4B, p3) twice, C4B, p1, place marker, m1, p1, m1, place marker, p1, (C4B, p3) twice, C4B, p2. (45 sts)

Row 10: patt to marker, sm, k to marker, sm, patt to end.

Row 11: patt to marker, sm, m1, p to marker, m1, sm, patt to end. (47 sts)

Repeat last 2 rows three more times, until there are 11 sts between markers. (53 sts)

Patt 1 row.

Row 19: Patt to marker, remove marker, place 11 sts from between markers on holder, cast on 1 st, remove marker, patt to end. (43 sts)

Continue in pattern until mitten measures 11cm/4¼in from cast on edge, ending on row 10.

All sizes

Next row: p2, *ssk, k2tog, p3(2:3), repeat from * three(five:five) times, ssk, k2tog, p2. (21(26:31) sts)

Next row: k2, *p2, k3(2:3), repeat from * three(five:five) times, p2, k2.

Next row: p2tog, *C2B, p2tog, p1(0:1), repeat from * three(five:five) times, C2B, p2tog. (16(19:24) sts)

Next row: k1, *p2, k2tog, k1, k2tog, repeat from * three(five:five) times, p2, k1. (10(8:14) sts)

Next row: (k2tog) to end. (5(4:7) sts)

Break yarn and follow *Sewing up* instructions on page 6.

Thumb, size 6–12 months only

Place 11 sts from holder onto a 3mm (UK 11/US 2) needle.

With RS facing, using camel yarn and 3mm (UK 11/US 2) needles, pick up and purl 1 st from thumb gap before sts on needles; purl 11 sts from needle, pick up and purl 1 st from gap. (13 sts)

Work 4 rows in rev st st.

Next row: (ssk) three times, k1, (k2tog) three times. (7 sts)

Break yarn, leaving a long tail, and thread through remaining sts, pull tight and secure. Sew up side of thumb.

Snowflake

Materials:

Baby – between 4-ply (fingering) and DK (US sport) weight yarn
Yarn A: 1 x 50g (1.75oz) ball, cream
Yarn B: small amount, aqua

2 stitch markers

Stitch holder

Needles:

2 pairs – 3.25mm (UK 10/US 3) and 3.5mm (UK 10/US 4) needles

Tapestry (blunt-end) needle for sewing up

Tension:

25 sts x 32 rows = 10cm/4in over st st using 3.5mm (UK 10/US 4) needles

Chart:

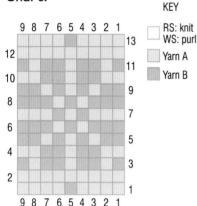

KEY

☐ RS: knit
WS: purl

▨ Yarn A

▦ Yarn B

Instructions:

Knitted flat.

Make two.

Cast on 25(29:33) sts using yarn B and 3.25mm (UK 10/US 3) needles.

Change to yarn A.

Row 1: k1, (p1, k1) to end.

Row 2: p1, (k1, p1) to end.

Repeat rows 1 and 2 twice more.

Change to 3.5mm (UK 10/US 4) needles.

Row 7 (RS): k.

Row 8: p.

Row 9: k1 in yarn B, (k1 in yarn A, k1 in yarn B) to end.

Row 10: p1 in yarn A, (p1 in yarn B, p1 in yarn A) to end.

Continue in st st for rest of pattern.

Sizes 0–3 months and 3–6 months only

Work 2 rows in st st using yarn A.

Starting with row 1 of Snowflake chart, work as follows:

Row 13: k2(3), work chart, k to end.

Row 14: p14(17), work chart, p to end.

Continue until all chart rows are complete.

Work 1(3) row(s) in st st using yarn A.

Size 6–12 months only

Continue in yarn A.

Row 11: k16, place marker, m1, k1, m1, place marker, k to end. (35 sts)

Row 12: p to marker, sm, p to marker, p to end.

Starting with row 1 of Snowflake chart, work as follows:

Row 13: k4, work chart, k to marker, sm, m1, k to marker, m1, sm, k to end. (37 sts)

Row 14: p to marker, sm, p to marker, sm, p3, work chart, p to end.

Repeat last 2 rows three more times, until there are 11 sts between markers. (43 sts)

Next row: k4, work chart, k to marker, remove marker; place 11 sts from between markers on holder, cast on 1 st, remove marker, k to end. (33 sts)

Continue in pattern until chart is complete.

Work 5 rows in st st using yarn A.

All sizes

Continue in yarn A only.

Next row: k2(2:3), (ssk) twice, k1(3:3), (k2tog) twice, k3(3:5), (ssk) twice, k1(3:3), (k2tog) twice, k2(2:3). (17(21:25) sts)

Next row: p.

Next row: k2, ssk(ssk:ssk twice), k1(3:1), k2tog(k2tog:k2tog twice), k3, ssk(ssk:ssk twice), k1(3:1), k2tog(k2tog:k2tog twice), k2. (13(17:17) sts)

Next row: (p2tog) three(four:four) times, p1, (p2tog) three(four:four) times. (7(9:9) sts)

Break yarn and follow *Sewing up* instructions on page 6.

Thumb, size 6–12 months only

Place 11 sts from holder onto a 3.5mm (UK 10/US 3) needle.

With RS facing, using yarn A and 3.5mm (UK 10/US 3) needles, pick up and knit 1 st from thumb gap before sts on needles; knit 11 sts from needle, pick up and knit 1 st from gap. (13 sts)

Work 3 rows in st st.

Next row: (ssk) three times, k1, (k2tog) three times. (7 sts)

Break yarn, leaving a long tail, and thread through remaining sts, pull tight and secure. Sew up side of thumb.

Spotted Pony

Materials:

Baby – between 4-ply (fingering) and DK (US sport)
 weight yarn
 Yarn A: 1 x 50g (1.75oz) ball, mid-brown
 Yarn B: small amount, cream

2 stitch markers

Stitch holder

Needles:

2 pairs – 3mm (UK 11/US 2) and 3.25mm (UK 10/
 US 3) needles

Tapestry (blunt-end) needle for sewing up

Tension:

25 sts x 34 rows = 10cm/4in over st st using 3.25mm
 (UK 10/US 3) needles

Chart:

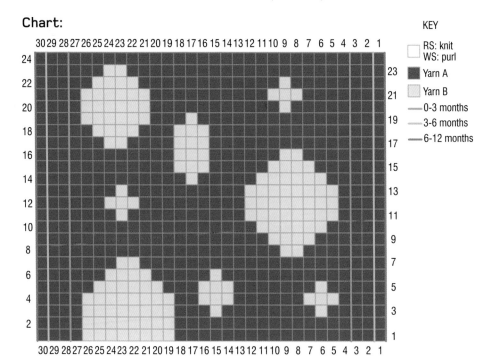

KEY

	RS: knit
	WS: purl
■	Yarn A
▨	Yarn B
—	0-3 months
—	3-6 months
—	6-12 months

Instructions:

Knitted flat.

Make two.

Cast on 25(29:31) sts using yarn A and 3mm (UK 11/
US 2) needles.

Row 1: k1, (p1, k1) to end.

Row 2: p1, (k1, p1) to end.

Rows 3–6: repeat rows 1 and 2 twice more.

Row 7: repeat row 1.

Row 8: rib 11(13:14) as set, k2tog, rib to end.
(24(28:30 sts)

Change to 3.25mm (UK 10/US 3) needles and continue in
st st for rest of pattern.

Sizes 0–3 months and 3–6 months only

Starting with a k row and row 1 of Spotted Pony chart, work
in st st until 20(22) chart rows are complete, ending with a
purl row.

Size 6–12 months only

Starting with a k row and row 1 of Spotted Pony chart, work
as follows:

Row 9: patt 15, place marker, m1 in yarn A, place marker,
patt to end. (31 sts)

Row 10: patt to marker, sm, p to marker in yarn A, sm, patt to end.

Row 11: patt to marker, sm, m1, k to marker in yarn A, m1, sm, patt to end. (33 sts).

Repeat last 2 rows four more times, until there are 11 sts between markers. (41 sts)

Work 1 row.

Next row: patt to marker, remove marker, place 11 sts from between markers on holder, remove marker, patt to end. (30 sts)

Continue in st st until 24 chart rows are complete, ending with purl row.

All sizes

Continue in yarn A.

Next row: k2 (ssk) twice, k1(3:3), (k2tog) twice, k2(2:4), (ssk) twice, k1(3:3), (k2tog) twice, K2. (16(20:22) sts)

Next row: p.

Next row: k2(2:1), ssk(ssk:ssk twice), k1(3:1), k2tog(k2tog:k2tog twice), k2, ssk(ssk:ssk twice), k1(3:1), k2tog(k2tog:k2tog twice), k2(2:1). (12(16:14) sts)

Next row: (p2tog) to end. (6(8:7) sts)

Break yarn and follow *Sewing up* instructions on page 6.

Thumb, size 6–12 months only

Place 11 sts from holder onto a 3.25mm (UK 10/US 3) needle.

With RS facing, using yarn A and 3.25mm (UK 10/US 3) needles, pick up and knit 1 st from thumb gap before sts on needles; knit 11 sts from needle, pick up and knit 1 st from gap. (13 sts)

Work 3 rows in st st.

Next row: (ssk) three times, k1, (k2tog) three times. (7 sts)

Break yarn, leaving a long tail, and thread through remaining sts, pull tight and secure. Sew up side of thumb.

Strawberry

Materials:

Baby – between 4-ply (fingering) and DK (US sport) weight yarn
Yarn A: 1 x 50g (1.75oz) ball, red
Yarn B: small amount, cream
Yarn C: small amount, lime

2 stitch markers

Stitch holder

Needles:

2 sets – 3mm (UK 11/US 2) and 3.25mm (UK 10/US 3) DPN, or a 3mm (UK 11/US 2) and 3.25mm (UK 10/US 3) circular needle

Tapestry (blunt-end) needle for sewing up

Tension:

25 sts x 34 rounds = 10cm/4in over st st using 3.25mm (UK 11/US 3) needles

Seed pattern:

Rounds 1 and 2: k.

Round 3: (k1 in yarn A, k1 in yarn B, k2 in yarn A) rep to end.

Rounds 4–6: k in yarn A.

Round 7: (k3 in yarn A, k1 in yarn B) to end.

Round 8: k in yarn A.

Instructions:

These mittens are worked in the round using either double-pointed needles, or a circular needle and the magic loop method.

Make two.

Cast on 24(28:32) sts in yarn A and 3mm (UK 11/US 2) DPN or a 3mm (UK 11/US 2) circular needle, then join in the round, taking care not to twist stitches.

Round 1: (k2, p2) to end.

Repeat round 1 seven(seven:nine) more times.

Change to 3.25mm (UK 10/US 3) DPN or a 3.25mm (UK 10/US 3) circular needle.

Sizes 0–3 months and 3–6 months only

Work in seed pattern until mitten measures 9.5(11.5)cm/3¾(4½)in from cast-on edge.

Size 6–12 months only

Work 2 rounds in seed pattern.

Continue in seed pattern as follows:

Round 13: patt 16, place marker, m1, place marker, patt to end. (33 sts)

Round 14: patt to marker, sm, k to markers in yarn A only, sm, patt to end.

Round 15: patt to marker, sm, m1, k to marker in yarn A, m1, sm, patt to end. (35 sts)

Round 16: patt to marker, sm, k to markers in yarn A only, sm, patt to end.

Repeat last 2 rounds four more times, until there are 11 sts between markers. (43 sts)

Next round: patt to marker, remove marker, place 11 sts from between markers on holder, remove marker, patt to end. (32 sts)

Continue in seed pattern until mitten measures 13cm/5in from cast-on edge.

All sizes

Continue in seed pattern.

Next round: (k2, k2tog) to end. (18(21:24) sts)

Next round: k.

Next round: (k1, k2tog) to end. (12(14:16) sts)

Next round: (k2tog) to end. (6(7:8) sts)

Break yarn and follow *Sewing up* instructions on page 6.

Thumb, size 6–12 months only

Place 11 sts from holder onto a 3.25mm (UK 10/US 3) DPN or a 3.25mm (UK 10/US 3) circular needle.

With RS facing, using yarn A, pick up and knit 1 st from thumb gap before sts on needle/s; knit 11 sts from needle, pick up and knit 1 st from gap. (13 sts)

Work 3 more rounds.

Next round: (ssk) three times, k1, (k2tog) three times. (7 sts)

Break yarn, leaving a long tail, and thread through remaining sts, pull tight and secure. Sew up side of thumb.

Leaf section
Make two.

*Cast on 1 st. Using yarn C and 3mm(3mm:3.25mm) (UK 11/US 2:UK 11/US 2:UK 10/US 3) needles and knit flat as follows:

Row 1 (RS): kfb. (2 sts)

Row 2: p.

Row 3: k1, m1, k1. (3 sts)

Row 4: p.

Row 5: k1, m1, k1, m1, k1. (5 sts)

Row 6: p.

Row 7: k.

Row 8: p.

Row 9: k1, m1, k3, m1, k1. (7 sts)

Break yarn and place 7 sts on holder.

Repeat from * three more times to make a total of 4 leaves.

Place the four sets of 7 sts from holder onto one 3mm(3mm:3.25mm) (UK 11/US 2:UK 11/US 2:UK 10/US 3) DPN, or a 3mm(3mm:3.25mm) (UK 11/US 2:UK 11/US 2:UK 10/US 3) circular needle. (28 sts)

With RS facing, using yarn C, knit across all 28 sts and join in the round, taking care not to twist stitches, k1 and place marker for start of round. (28 sts)

Round 11: (k5, k2tog) to end. (24 sts)

Round 12: k.

Round 13: (k2, k2tog) to end. (18 sts)

Round 14: k.

Round 15: (k1, k2tog) to end. (12 sts)

Round 16: (k2tog) to end. (6 sts)

Break yarn and follow *Sewing up* instructions on page 6.

To make up all sizes

Using the photo for guidance, place leaf section over top of mitten and, using yarn C and a back stitch, stitch down from the top centre of the leaf section to the top of each leaf joint; do this also from the top centre to the bottom of each leaf point.

Repeat with the other leaf section.

Stripes

Materials:

Baby – between 4-ply (fingering) and DK (US sport) weight yarn
- Yarn A: small amount, cream
- Yarn B: small amount, aqua
- Yarn C: small amount, lilac
- Yarn D: small amount, lime

2 stitch markers

Stitch holder

Needles:

2 pairs – 3mm (UK 11/US 2) and 3.25mm (UK 10/US 3) needles

Tapestry (blunt-end) needle for sewing up

Tension:

25 sts x 34 rows = 10cm/4in over st st using 3.25mm (UK 10/US 3) needles

Instructions:

Knitted flat.

Make two.

Cast on 24(28:32) sts in yarn A and 3mm (UK 11/US 2) needles.

Row 1: k1,(p2, k2) to last 3 sts, p2, k1.

Row 2: p1, (k2, p2) to last 3 sts, k2, p1.

Repeat rows 1 and 2 twice more.

Change to 3.25mm (UK 10/US 3) needles.

Row 7: change to yarn B, k12(24:16), m1, k to end. (25(29:33) sts)

Row 8: p.

Starting with a knit row, continue in st st for rest of pattern, working stripes as follows: 2 rows in yarn C, 2 rows in yarn D, 2 rows in yarn A, 2 rows in yarn B.

Sizes 0–3 months and 3–6 months only

Work as set until 22(24) stripe rows are complete, ending with a purl row.

Size 6–12 months only

Keeping stripe pattern correct, work thumb increases as follows:

Row 9: k16, place marker, m1, k1, m1, place marker, k to end. (35 sts)

Row 10: p to marker, sm, p to marker, p to end.

Row 11: k to marker, sm, m1, k to marker, m1, sm, k to end. (37 sts)

Repeat last 2 rows three more times, until there are 11 stitches between markers. (43 sts)

Row 18: p.

Row 19: k to marker, remove marker, place 11 sts from between markers on holder, cast on 1 st, k to end. (33 sts)

Continue in stripe pattern until 26 stripe rows are complete, ending with a purl row.

All sizes

Continue in stripe pattern as follows:

Next row: *k2(2:3), (ssk) twice, k2(3:3), (k2tog) twice, k1(1:2), repeat from * once more, k1. (19(23:27) sts)

Next row: p.

Next row: k2, ssk(ssk:ssk twice), k2(3:1), k2tog(k2tog:k2tog twice), k3, ssk(ssk:ssk twice), k1(3:1), k2tog(k2tog:k2tog twice), k2. (15(19:19) sts)

Next row: (p2tog) three(four:four) times, p3tog, (p2tog) three(four:four) times. (7(9:9) sts)

Break yarn and follow *Sewing up* instructions on page 6.

Thumb, size 6–12 months only

Place 11 sts from holder onto a 3.25mm (UK 10/US 3) needle.

With RS facing, using yarn C and 3.25mm (UK 10/US 3) needles, pick up and knit 1 st from thumb gap before sts on needles; knit 11 sts from needle, pick up and knit 1 st from gap. (13 sts)

Work 3 rows in st st, keeping stripes correct.

Next row: (ssk) three times, k1, (k2tog) three times. (7 sts)

Break yarn, leaving a long tail, and thread through remaining sts, pull tight and secure. Sew up side of thumb.

Tweed

Materials:

4-ply (fingering) weight yarn
  Yarn A: 1 x 50g (1.75oz) ball, aqua
  Yarn B: 1 x 50g (1.75oz) ball, cream

2 stitch markers

Stitch holder

Needles:

2 sets – 2.75mm (UK 12/US 2) and 3mm (UK 11/
  UK 2) DPN, or 2.75mm (UK 12/US 2) and 3mm
  (UK 11/UK 2) circular needles

Tapestry (blunt-end) needle for sewing up

Tension:

28 sts x 60 rounds = 10cm/4in over st st using 3mm
  (UK 11/US 2) needles

Instructions:

These mittens are worked in the round using either double-pointed needles, or a circular needle and the magic loop method.

Make two.

Cast on 28(32:36) sts using yarn A and 2.75mm (UK 12/US 2) DPN or a 2.75mm (UK 12/US 2) circular needle, then join in the round, taking care not to twist stitches.

Change to yarn B.

Round 1: (k2, p2) to end.

Repeat round 1 six more times.

Change to 3mm (UK 11/US 2) DPN or a 3mm (UK 11/US 2) circular needle and continue in tweed pattern as follows:

Round 8: using yarn A, (k1, p1) to end.

Round 9: using yarn B, (k1, sl1) to end.

Round 10: using yarn B, (p1, k1) to end.

Round 11: using yarn A, (sl1, k1) to end.

Sizes 0–3 months and 3–6 months only

Repeat rounds 8–11 nine(ten) more times.

Size 6–12 months only

Repeat rounds 8–11 once more.

Continue in tweed pattern as set by rounds 8–11, and start thumb shaping:

Round 16: patt 16, place marker, m1, place marker, patt to end. (37 sts)

Round 17: patt to marker, sm, patt to marker, sm, patt to end.

Round 18: patt to marker, sm, m1, patt to marker, m1, sm, patt to end. (39 sts)

Round 19: patt to marker, sm, patt to marker, sm, patt to end.

Repeat last 2 rounds five more times, until there are 13 sts between markers. (49 sts)

Round 30: patt to marker, remove marker, place 13 sts from between markers on holder, remove marker, patt to end. (36 sts)

Continue to work in tweed pattern until a total of 56 tweed rounds are complete.

All sizes

Next round: using yarn A, k1(0:1), p1(0:1), (k1, p2tog, k1, p1, k2tog, p1) three(four:four) times, k2tog(0:k2tog). (21(24:27) sts)

Next round: using yarn B, (k1, sl1) to last 1(0:1) st, k1(0:1).

Next round: using yarn B, (p1, k2tog) to end. (14(16:18) sts)

Next round: using yarn A, (k2tog) to end. 7(8:9) sts)

Break yarn and follow *Sewing up* instructions in page 6.

Thumb, size 6–12 months only

Place 13 sts from holder onto 3mm (UK 11/US 2) DPN or a 3mm (UK 11/US 2) circular needle.

With RS facing, and using yarn B, pick up and knit 1 st from thumb gap before sts on needle/s; knit 13 sts from needle and arrange in the round. (14 sts)

Change to yarn A and k two rounds.

Change to yarn B and k two rounds.

Change to yarn A and k one round.

Next row: (ssk) three times, (k2tog) four times. (7 sts)

Break yarn leaving a long tail and thread through rem sts, pull tight and secure. Weave in ends

Tiger Stripes

Materials:

Baby – between 4-ply (fingering) and DK (US sport)
weight yarn
Yarn A: 1 x 50g (1.75oz) ball, cream
Yarn B: 1 x 50g (1.75oz) ball, amber

2 stitch markers

Stitch holder

Needles:

2 pairs – 3mm (UK 11/US 2) and 3.25mm (UK 10/
US 3) needles

Tapestry (blunt-end) needle for sewing up

Tension:

25 sts x 34 rows = 10cm/4in over st st using 3.25mm
(UK 10/US 3) needles

Chart:

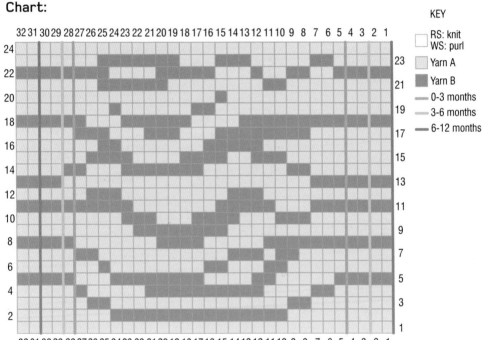

KEY

RS: knit
WS: purl

Yarn A

Yarn B

— 0-3 months
— 3-6 months
— 6-12 months

Instructions:

Knitted flat.

Make two.

Cast on 24(28:32) sts in yarn A and 3mm (UK 11/
US 2) needles.

Row 1: (k1, p1) to end.

Repeat row 1 four(five:six) more times

Change to 3.25mm (UK 10/US 3) needles and continue
in st st, starting with a knit row and working row 1 of Tiger
Stripes chart as set.

Size 0-3 months and 3-6 months only

Continue until 20(22) chart rows are complete.

Size 6-12 months only

Work one more chart row.

Row 3: work 16 sts of chart, place marker, m1 in yarn A,
place marker, 16 sts of chart. (33 sts)

Row 4: work 16 sts of chart, sm, p to marker in yarn B, sm,
work 16 sts of chart.

Row 5: work 16 sts of chart, sm, m1, k to marker in yarn A,
m1, sm, work 16 sts of chart. (35 sts)

Repeat last 2 rows four more times, keeping thumb stripes
correct, until there are 11 sts between markers. (43 sts)

Repeat row 4 one more time.

Next row: work 16 sts of chart, remove marker, place 11 sts from between markers on holder, remove marker, work 16 sts of chart. (32 sts)

Continue in st st until 24 chart rows are complete.

All sizes

Continue in yarn A only.

Next row: (k2, k2tog) to end. (18(21:24) sts)

Next row: p.

Next row: (k1, k2tog) to end. (12(14:16) sts)

Next row: p2tog to end.

Break yarn and follow *Sewing up* instructions on page 6.

Thumb, size 6–12 months only

Place 11 sts from holder onto a 3.25mm (UK 10/ US 3) needle.

With RS facing, using yarn A and 3.25mm (UK 10/US 3) needles, pick up and knit 1 st from thumb gap before sts on needles; knit 11 sts from needle, pick up and knit 1 st from gap. (13 sts)

Row 2: using yarn B, p to end.

Row 3: using yarn A, k to end.

Row 4: using yarn B, p to end.

Row 5: using yarn A, (ssk) three times, k1, (k2tog) three times. (7 sts)

Break yarn, leaving a long tail, and thread through remaining sts, pull tight and secure. Sew up side of thumb.

Acknowledgements

Thank you to Katie French for commissioning the
book, and to Emily Adam for her editing skills.
A thank you to Bronagh Miskelly for the pattern
writing and to my team of knitters.
Also a big thank you to the yarn companies
that kindly provided the yarns; Laughing Hens for the
Rooster yarn, Designer Yarns for the
Debbie Bliss yarn, Patons and Rowan.